my guide to money

Jobs and Money

Lemonade 25¢

Published in the United States of America by Cherry Lake Publishing
Ann Arbor, Michigan
www.cherrylakepublishing.com

Content Adviser: Danielle Peart, CPA
Reading Adviser: Cecilia Minden, PhD, Literacy expert and children's author
Book Design: Jennifer Wahi
Illustrator: Jeff Bane

Photo Credits: © Sergey Novikov/Shutterstock.com, 5; © N_Sakarin/Shutterstock.com, 7; © Andrey_Popov/
Shutterstock.com, 9; © ESB Professional/Shutterstock.com, 11; © Antonio Guillem/Shutterstock.com, 13;
© Monkey Business Images/Shutterstock.com, 15; © nito/ Shutterstock.com, 17; © wavebreakmedia/
Shutterstock.com, 19; © Eakachai Leesin/Shutterstock.com, 21; © KPG Payless2/Shutterstock.com, 23;
Cover, 1, 6, 14, 20, Jeff Bane

Library of Congress Cataloging-in-Publication Data

Names: Colby, Jennifer, 1971- author.
Title: Jobs and money / by Jennifer Colby.
Description: Ann Arbor : Cherry Lake Publishing, [2018] | Series: My guide to
    money | Includes bibliographical references and index.
Identifiers: LCCN 2018003318| ISBN 9781534128972 (hardcover) | ISBN
    9781534130678 (pdf) | ISBN 9781534132177 (pbk.) | ISBN 9781534133877
    (hosted ebook)
Subjects: LCSH: Wages--Juvenile literature. | Money--Juvenile literature.
Classification: LCC HD4909 .C535 2018 | DDC 331.2/1--dc23
LC record available at https://lccn.loc.gov/2018003318

Printed in the United States of America
Corporate Graphics

About the author: Jennifer Colby is a school librarian in Michigan. She gets paid a salary for her work.

About the illustrator: Jeff Bane and his two business partners own a studio along the American River in Folsom, California, home of the 1849 Gold Rush. When Jeff's not sketching or illustrating for clients, he's either swimming or kayaking in the river to relax.

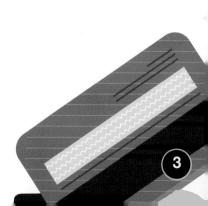

3

Do you help clean the house? Do the dishes? Those jobs are **chores**. Most people have jobs.

A job is work. It pays money.

Most jobs give you a **paycheck**.

There are different types of paid jobs.

A job can pay a **salary**. A salary is a **fixed** sum of money.

What job do you want?

Jobs in offices often pay salaries. You can take time off and still get paid.

There is another way to get paid. A job can pay by the hour. This is an **hourly wage**.

Workers at stores sometimes get paid hourly.

How would you like to be paid?

Hourly workers don't get paid if they do not work.

Do you want a job? Ask an adult how you can make money. You could walk dogs. You could have a yard sale. What else could you do?

glossary

chores (CHOHRZ) small jobs done around the house

fixed (FIKST) does not change

hourly wage (OUR-lee WAYJ) the money paid per hour for work done

paycheck (PAY-chek) a check that pays someone for work done

salary (SAL-ur-ee) the fixed amount of money someone is paid for a job

index